Guitar Styles from Around the Globe

National Guitar

GH00381308

Your passport to a new world of music

BANNING EYRE

Alfred, the leader in educational publishing,

and the National Guitar Workshop,

one of America's finest guitar schools, have joined

forces to bring you the best, most progressive

educational tools possible. We hope you will enjoy

this book and encourage you to look for

other fine products from Alfred and the

National Guitar Workshop.

Alfred Publishing Co., Inc.
16320 Roscoe Blvd., Suite 100
P.O. Box 10003
Van Nuys, CA 91410-0003
alfred.com

ISBN-10: 0-7390-2474-4
ISBN-13: 978-0-7390-2474-4

This book was acquired, edited and produced
by Workshop Arts, Inc., the publishing arm of

...itor

...Northford, CT

...ost respected griot guitarists in
...of the top traditional singers,
...ative electric guitarist and arranger.

Contents

0
Track 1

A compact disc is included with this book. This disc can make learning with the book easier and more enjoyable. The symbol shown at the left appears next to every example that is on the CD. Use the CD to help ensure that you're capturing the feel of the examples, interpreting the rhythms correctly, and so on. The track number below the symbol corresponds directly to the example you want to hear. Track 1 will help you tune your guitar to this CD.

Have fun!

About the Author

Banning Eyre has played guitar professionally since the mid-1970s, working in genres as diverse as jazz, flamenco, dance-rock, and reggae. Since 1990, he has specialized in guitar styles from Africa, making six trips to the continent to research guitar music. Over the years, Banning has played in a series of Congolese soukous bands in Boston, in the West African folk ensemble Cora Connection, and with a variety of musicians performing Zimbabwean mbira music. He teaches African guitar styles, both privately and in workshops at Tribal Soundz in New York City.

During travels in Africa, Banning has performed with the Super Rail Band of Bamako and Sali Sidibe in Mali, and with Thomas Mapfumo and the Blacks Unlimited in Zimbabwe. He plays on two Thomas Mapfumo albums, "Chimurenga '98" and "Chimurenga Explosion," and on a track from Taj Mahal and Toumani Diabate's "Kulanjan" (Hannibal, 1999), voted the Folk Roots Album of the Year in the UK.

Banning has written about international music, especially African guitar styles, since 1988. He comments and reports on music for National Public Radio's *All Things Considered* and contributes regularly to the *Boston Phoenix, Guitar Player, Rhythm, Folk Roots, The Beat, CMJ New Music Monthly,* and the *Music Hound* and *All Music Guide* series of books. He has traveled extensively in Africa and produces regular programs for the public radio series *Afropop Worldwide*.

In 1995, Banning coauthored *AFROPOP!: An Illustrated Guide to Contemporary African Music* with Sean Barlow. His critically acclaimed book *In Griot Time: An American Guitarist in Mali* (Temple University Press, 2000) recounts his seven-month apprenticeship with Djelimady Tounkara of the Super Rail Band of Bamako, Mali. He compiled a companion CD, *In Griot Time: String Music from Mali* (Stern's Africa, 2000), including a number of his own recordings of musicians in Mali. Banning is currently at work on a book about Thomas Mapfumo and the contemporary history of Zimbabwe.

Banning is the senior editor at **www.afropop.org**. You can contact him and learn more about his work by visiting **www.banningeyre.com**.

Pronunciation Guide

Amponsah	=	am-POHN-sah
Balafon	=	BAH-lah-fohn
Chimurenga	=	CHI-mur-EHNG-ah
Clave	=	CLAH-vay
Diaoura	=	jah-OO-rah
Dosongoni	=	DOH-soh-NGOH-nee
Griot	=	GREE-oh
Guitare etouffée	=	gih-TAHR AY-too-fay
Hosho	=	HOH-shoh
Kaira	=	KIE-rah
Kamelengoni	=	KAH-meh-leh-NGOH-nee
Karigamombe	=	KAH-ree-gah-MOHM-bay
Karagnan	=	KAH-ran-YAH(n)
Keme Burema	=	KAY-may BRAH-mah
Kwaito	=	KWIE-toh
Kwassa-kwassa	=	KWAH-sah KWAH-sah
Marabi	=	mah-RAH-bee
Marche militaire	=	MARZH mee-lee-TEHR
Marovany	=	MAH-roh-VAHN
Matonge	=	MAH-tohn-gay
Mbaqanga	=	mbah-KAHN-gah
Mbira dza vadzimu	=	MBEE-rah DZAH-vah-DZEE-moo
Mi-solo	=	MEE-soh-loh
Ngoni	=	NGOH-nee
Pidigori	=	PIH-dee-goh-ree
Seben	=	SEH-ben
Son montuno	=	SOHN mahn-TOON-oh
Songhai	=	SOHN-gie
Soukous	=	SOO-koos
Sungura	=	soon-GOO-rah
Sunjata	=	soon-JAH-tah
Taireva	=	tie-RAY-vah
Ukapika	=	OO-kah-PEE-kah
Valiha	=	vah-LEE
Wassoulou	=	WAH-soo-loo
Yoruba	=	yoh-ROO-bah

Introduction

African guitar is a big subject, as big as the continent itself. Africa is 54 countries and many hundreds of distinct ethnic groups, and while most people think of African music as principally drumming and singing, there is an astounding number of guitar styles unique to particular African settings. Paul Simon's breakthrough 1986 album "Graceland" focused international attention on South African pop music and initiated a process of discovery for curious music fans around the world. What they found was the dazzling array of music styles we now call *Afropop*. From the tangled guitar boogie of the Congo—*soukous* music—to the serene percussive weave of Nigerian *juju* music, to the flashy fingerpickers of Mali and Madagascar, Africa's treasure chest of beautiful and original contemporary guitar idioms seems inexhaustible.

Many of these idioms deserve a book of their own. Some are extensions of ancient musical traditions that used indigenous instruments for centuries before the first guitars came to Africa with Portuguese sailors in the 16th century. These "roots" genres sometimes have rich, widely interpreted repertoires and diverse, demanding techniques specifically developed to render the sounds of African instruments on guitar. Even brazenly modern guitar styles, like those in the Congo, have achieved a remarkable level of depth and rigor within a few short decades of development. For all the travel and study I've put in, I've only scratched the surface of Africa's guitar wealth. But I've learned enough to convey a number of important principles of some key African guitar styles.

That is the limited objective of *Guitar Atlas: Africa*. The African guitar styles introduced here are by no means the only ones worthy of study. They are simply the ones I have been fortunate enough to discover, and the ones I've become intrigued enough to tackle as a player. This book would not have been possible without the openness and generosity of the many guitarists who have shared their wisdom with me. Using the principles and fundamentals in this book as a starting point, players will be able to approach recordings of African music with greater appreciation and understanding. Still, there is no substitute for sitting down with those who grew up playing these styles, especially if you can do so in Africa. My fondest hope for this book is that it will inspire other players to dig deeper into this underexamined world of guitar music. I hope others will make their own journeys, write their own books and articles, and bring as yet undiscovered African guitar geniuses to international attention.

Guitar Atlas: Africa assumes that you have some experience playing and reading standard music notation and/or TAB, and that you have some experience with both fingerstyle and flatpick playing. It also assumes that you have some understanding of basic music theory—time signatures, rhythms and note values (ranging from whole notes to sixteenth notes), intervals, harmony (chords and chord symbols), and so on.

Chapter 1   PALM WINE PICKERS

TWO-FINGER PICKING

Portuguese sailors likely brought the first guitars to west Africa. By the late 19th and early 20th centuries, guitarists could be found in many west and central African port cities playing in a recognizable style. Right-hand picking was all done with the thumb and index finger, often playing together, sometimes staggering the rhythm to give it a decidedly African lilt.

Picking hand of **Djelimady Tounkara**, *(born 1947), master griot guitarist of Mali*

Throughout the 20th century, fledgling African guitarists have typically learned to play on homemade instruments, such as this Zimbabwean "oil-tin" guitar.

PALM WINE BASICS

The Kru people of Sierra Leone were sailors who often spent time in foreign cities and played an important role in disseminating the so-called *palm wine* guitar style. The name refers to the milky alcoholic beverage favored in local bars where guitar-playing sailors would perform informally. Palm wine guitar became a generally west African musical genre that had its heyday in the mid-20th century. Sierra Leone produced one of the greatest palm wine guitarists, S. E. Rogie (1926–1994). Rogie's only surviving peer is Daniel Amponsah (a.k.a. Ko Nimo) of Ghana. Ko Nimo has merged the style with jazz and classical guitar. He starts students off with the simple exercise in example 1.

Ko Nimo *(born 1934) is generally acknowledged as the greatest living palm wine guitarist.*

p =	thumb
i =	index finger

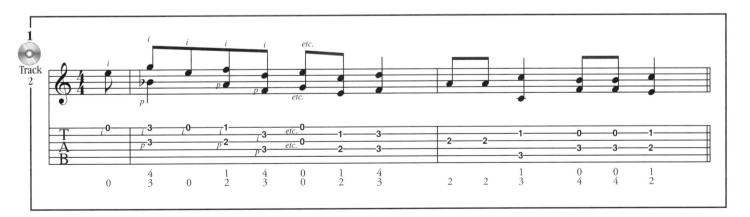

PARALLEL 6THS

You may have noticed the use of *parallel 6ths* (a series of harmonic 6ths played in sequence) in example 1, an important feature in many west and central African guitar styles. Here's another exercise to help you get comfortable with 6ths. Practice playing example 2 cleanly and smoothly so that each pair of notes rings until the next is struck. The sound should be very connected.

MAKING IT SWING

The key to all African guitar styles is rhythm. Finding just the right *syncopation* (accent shifted to a weak beat or weak part of a beat), the right feel, frequently makes all the difference. Example 3 is a Ko Nimo palm wine accompaniment in the style known as *amponsah*. It's based on the following bass line, which is played with the right thumb.

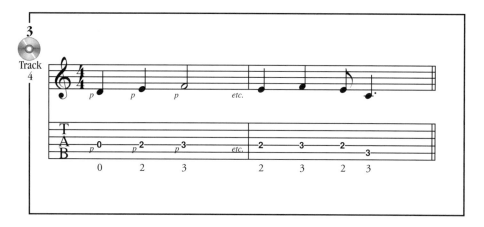

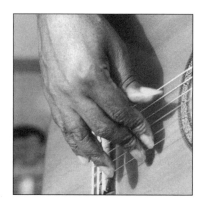

*A closeup of **Ko Nimo**'s picking hand. The guitarist's 1990 album "Osabarima" remains a landmark as the first CD recording of music by a Ghanaian artist.*

Now add some syncopation. Note that *p* should still pick the original line on the onbeats, but now it also plays answering notes on the offbeats (that is, the second sixteenth note of each beat). This creates a conversational effect, one of many call-and-response techniques found in African guitar. Notice how the occasional note picked with *i* adds an extra rhythmic element to the part. Be sure to observe the left-hand fingering, and let all the notes ring as long as possible.

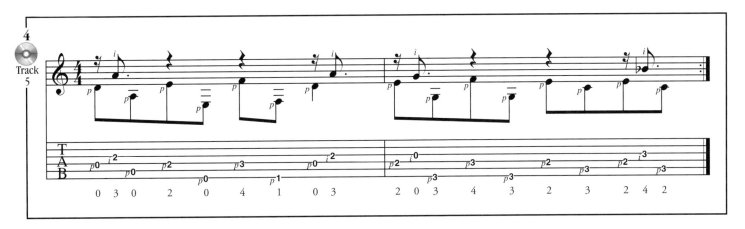

Finally, here are two variations. Each makes efficient use of just a few extra or changed notes. The first (example 5) adds a chromatic note (F♯) to the bass line, creating a little extra harmonic tension. The second (example 6) adds two melody notes to the first bar, suggesting the direction a melody line might take in a full-blown performance.

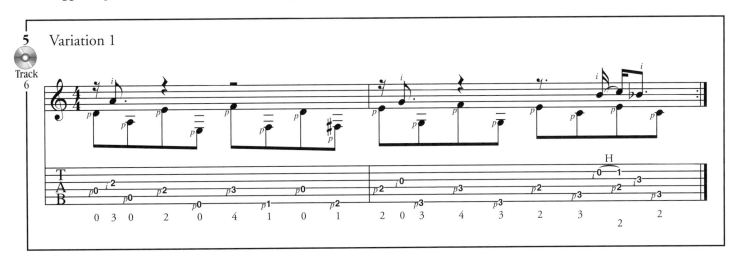

Chapter 2

HIGHLIFE AND JUJU

RHYTHM GUITAR

Palm wine guitar was the foundation of some important African pop styles. The most crucial one in west African music was *highlife,* which blossomed in Ghana and Nigeria in the 1950s and 1960s. Highlife is electric guitar–band music in which the guitar becomes a rhythm instrument, strummed with a flatpick. We'll focus on rhythm guitar here, and save melodic flatpicking for the more elaborate Congo music in Chapter 3. One highly influential element of highlife rhythm guitar is the use of a dominant 7th chord built on the tonic of the key—for example, A7 in the key of A. This chord functions as a *secondary dominant* (a dominant chord applied to a chord other than I)—in this case, the V7 of IV. In highlife, this chord is typically used as a way of leading a progression to (or back to) the IV chord, as in example 7.

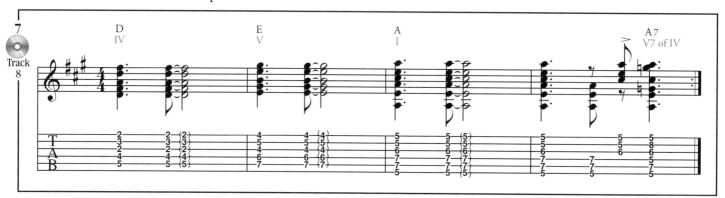

The rhythmic placement of this 7th chord is key. Falling between beats 3 and 4 of the measure, it comes as a surprise and creates a characteristic highlife effect.

Example 8 shows another fairly typical highlife chord progression. Play this against a strong, quarter-note bass-drum rhythm; start at a metronome setting of ♩ = 95 and increase the tempo as you become more comfortable. Highlife's signature swing comes in when a part like this is nestled in among a sizzling hi-hat part, a pumping bass line, and some tasty lead guitar, horns, and vocals. For variety, a song might break into a slower-changing progression, using a 7th chord to announce the change, as in measure 2. The following chord diagrams show which forms to use for example 8.

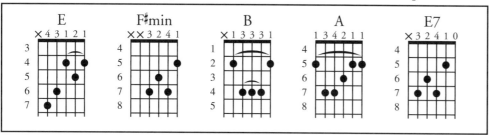

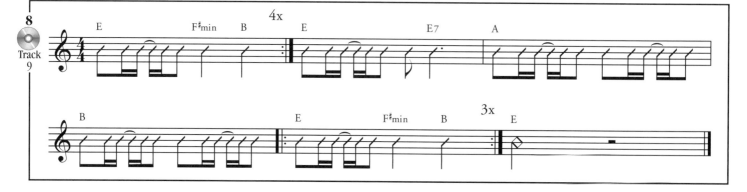

Often the guitarist in highlife plays chord progressions in arpeggios. Here's the basic progression from example 8 with the notes played individually. Be sure to keep the notes fingered throughout each chord for maximum resonance.

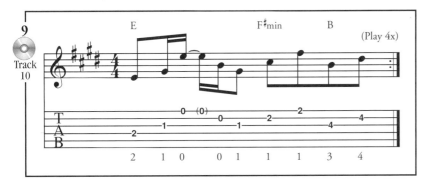

Finally, let's play a slightly longer progression that uses the same chord forms as in example 8, but with more complex strumming. Start example 10 slowly, until you're comfortable with the rhythm, and then work it up to ♩ = 120. The feel should be light and easy, even buoyant. Strum cleanly, but not hard. You can also add a nice effect by doing a quick half-step slide up into the first F♯min chord.

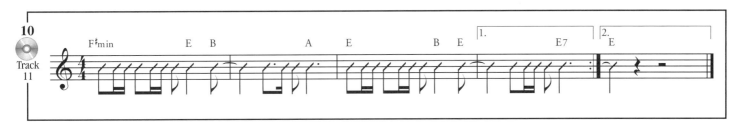

The African Brothers, formed in 1969, has come to be recognized as one of Ghana's classic highlife bands. Here, the group performs at an all-night "concert party," a combination of music and theatre.

JUJU MUSIC

Juju—a blend of palm wine guitar, highlife, and recreational percussion music of the *Yoruba* ethnic group—evolved in Nigeria starting in the 1920s. I. K. Dairo, Ebenezer Obey, and King Sunny Ade are among the best-known juju bandleaders. By the time KSA, as Ade is known, introduced juju to the world in the 1980s, the style's electric guitar arranging had taken on a distinctive character. In big juju bands like KSA's African Beats, guitars function almost like drums, locking relatively simple parts together to create textures that weave through the percussion. KSA's band has used up to five guitars, including KSA's own lead guitar, a pedal steel guitar, bass and two or three support guitars. Often the guitars come together to play tight, harmonized rhythmic melodies, especially at transition points, beginnings and endings.

Three guitar parts (and one drum part) combine in *Juju Slow* to create a fairly typical, relaxed juju groove. Start with the first rhythm guitar part. Once you've mastered that, try the second rhythm part, which uses a slightly different rhythm that locks in with the first. The notes on the last beat in this part are really just clicks, played with the strings muted on the fretting hand.

The lead part in *Juju Slow* is in the style of King Sunny Ade. Like the palm wine players, KSA plays with two fingers, *p* and *i*, and uses a lot of *double stops* (two notes played simultaneously by one player) like the ones in this piece. Try playing the lead an octave above where it's written—you'll be getting close to KSA's signature sound, high up on the neck of a solid-body guitar.

> = In a guitar part, strike the muted strings.

KSA signals his band using his guitar, much as the lead drummer in a traditional drumming ensemble would. Sometimes he uses a riff; sometimes, just by moving his capo, he tells the players that it's time to shift to another song without stopping. Example 11 is a typical signal riff. KSA might strum this with his busy thumb, but it's easier to play it with a flatpick.

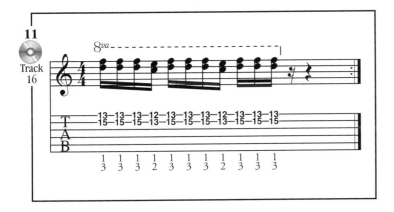

8va = *Ottava alta.* Play an octave higher than written.

King Sunny Ade (born 1946) is a pioneer of Nigerian juju music and one of the first African band leaders to tour successfully in Europe and the United States.

Chapter 3

CONGOLESE, RUMBA, AND SOUKOUS

The guitar-rich pop music of the Congo in central Africa has had more impact around the continent than any other Afropop genre. Beginning in the late 1940s, bands in Brazzaville and Kinshasa—cities that face each other across the Congo River—began fusing Cuban music with local sounds. By then, an important fingerpicking acoustic guitar tradition had taken shape in the Belgian Congo, championed by Jean Bosco Mwenda, a seminal figure in the development of guitar music throughout central and southern Africa. Mwenda's lilting style, which bears some resemblance to palm wine guitar, laid important groundwork for the brilliant electric guitarists who followed: Dr. Nico and Franco in the 1950s and 1960s, Manuaku Waku and Popolipo in the 1970s, and later, Diblo Dibala, Nene Tchakou, and others.

Urban, electric Congo music was first called *rumba* (named for the slow, Cuban-derived dance rhythm), though it more closely resembled the small-ensemble Cuban pop known as *son montuno* (also known as *son*). In Cuba, son had introduced prominent African rhythms and percussion into what had been more sedate, ballroom dance music. In Cuba and Puerto Rico, son became *salsa*. In Congo, it became African rumba, and as it incorporated rhythms from the vast Congolese interior, it earned new names: *soukous, kwassa-kwassa,* and *rumba rock.* Easily crossing ethnic and national barriers with its powerful dance rhythms, soukous became the disco music of Africa during the 1970s and 1980s.

Early rumba guitarists, especially the late, great Franco ("Sorcerer of the Guitar"), often played melodies in parallel 6ths, picking with *p* and *i* in much the way you learned on pages 5 and 6. Example 12 shows how you can create melodic passages in 6ths. Notice that you can alternate 6ths played on the 1st and 3rd, and 2nd and 4th strings.

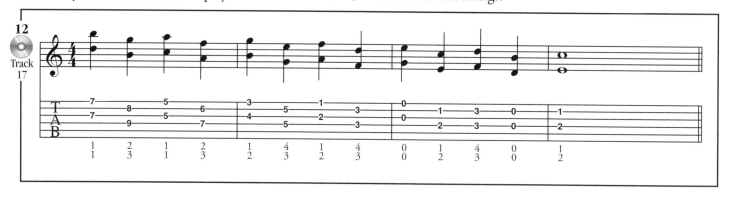

Manuaku Waku was the first lead guitarist for the pioneering rumba rock group Zaiko Langa Langa, formed in 1969. He later left to form his own group, Grand Zaiko Wawa.

THE CLAVE RHYTHM

The so-called *three-two clave* rhythm from Cuba is central to understanding Congo music. This rhythm, shown in example 13, uses a distinctive combination of three plus two (for a total of five) strokes. Clave was, of course, originally an African rhythm (as well an an instrument consisting of two sticks struck against one another), but it became the foundation of Cuban music, which in turn influenced pop styles around the world. Clave is cousin to the Bo Diddley beat, the rock backbeat, and New Orleans second-line music. Both Cuban and Congolese music involve layering rhythmic parts, but the clave rhythm is the key to everything.

Below is a fingerstyle guitar accompaniment that uses the clave rhythm in the bass part (notated with downward stems). It's important to feel the sensuous call-and-response character of this two-part rhythm, in which the two-stroke group always answers the three-stroke group. In most Congo guitar music, the clave is not as explicit as it is in example 13, but it's always implied.

When you become comfortable with clave, try embellishing it with parallel 6ths. If you can go into a melodic 6ths passage, and then return to the accompaniment in example 14, you'll understand the basics of Congo guitar music. Here's an example to try:

CONGOLESE RHYTHM GUITAR

As electric guitar became more prevalent in Congo music, the art of layering guitar parts developed. Almost all modern Congo guitarists use a pick, a notable exception being Franco, who played fingerstyle and was the champion of improvising melodies in 6ths. The remaining examples in this chapter are best played with a flatpick.

In Congo music, guitarists in a band rarely play the same part. Sometimes, a second or third guitar part will harmonize the first one, but guitarists usually play interlocking, complementary rhythms. Rhythm parts tend to be strong and straight, providing solid footing for syncopated rhythms in higher parts. A full soukous arrangement begins with a rumba section in which the harmony can be fairly complex, but as the song progresses into the second (mid-tempo) and final (fast) sections, the harmony often comes down to three chords.

The simple rhythm guitar part in *Matonge* is of a kind that would typically accompany mid-tempo singing in a soukous arrangement. Bass and bass drums would pump out the strong beats, so to make this part stand out a bit, guitarists emphasize the offbeats: one *and* two *and* three *and* four *and*.

Once you've mastered the rhythm part, take a look at the melody line. Notice the way that the phrases begin one sixteenth note after the downbeat, providing a rhythmic orientation that contrasts with and balances the rhythm part. Think of the two parts as playing two "sides" of the rhythm. The lead guitarist might play a part like this during the singing, when the goal is to create a groove to support harmonized, call-and-response vocals.

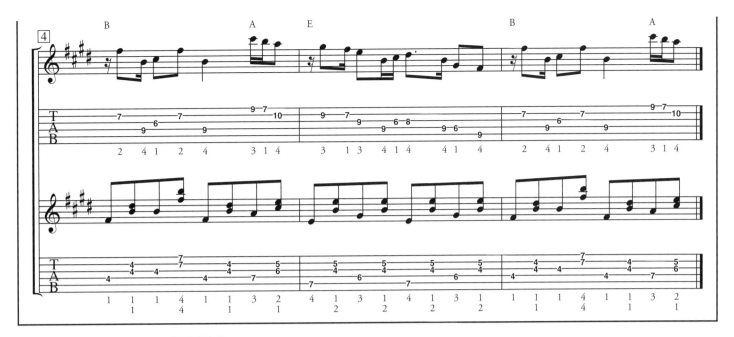

CONGOLESE LEAD GUITAR

Lead guitarists in Congolese music are renowned for speed, precision, and nimble finger work high on the fretboard. During the slow rumba or mid-tempo vocal portions of a song, the lead guitarist tends to play free-flowing melodies in response to the singers. But at a certain point in every soukous song, the drummer shifts to the final, high-energy *seben.* The clave rhythm moves to the snare drum, the singers switch to a rhythmic chanting section called the *animation,* and the guitars come forward in the texture; the high, cycling melodies of the lead guitar are especially prominent. The name "seben" reportedly comes from the English "seven." In the old days, listeners loved the dominant 7th chords introduced by the English-speaking, Ghanaian palm wine players. Shouting "Seven!" meant "Pull out the stops!"

Congo music is all about discipline. During a seben, the drummer signals changes. At each signal, all the guitarists change parts in a prearranged way, shifting to best complement the lead player's line. On pages 16–17, you'll find two sebens with lead, rhythm, *mi-solo* (third guitar), and bass parts. These sebens use a typical Congolese progression: I–IV–V–IV. Practice moving back and forth between the corresponding parts in both sebens. If you can work with other guitarists and a drummer, practice changing on cue from the drummer.

Popolipo Zanguila *played in Zaiko Langa Langa (formed in 1969) and a number of the group's spinoff bands, including Papa Wemba's original Viva la Musica and the Langa Langa Stars.*

SOUKOUS BASS

Bass parts in Congo music, which derive from hand-drum percussion, fill a strong rhythmic and harmonic role. Soukous music took shape during the heyday of the militaristic Mobutu regime (1965–1997), when the country was called Zaire. The aggressive bass style imitated the movement and attitude of Mobutu's soldiers and hence became known as *marche militaire.* This style of bass playing involves picking with *p* and *i,* creating a toggling effect between low and high lines. The sebens on pages 16 and 17 include classic marche militaire bass lines.

Diblo Dibala *became one of the most celebrated Congolese guitarists of the 1980s through his work with Kanda Bongo Man and, later, the group Loketo.*

CONGOLESE SEBEN 1

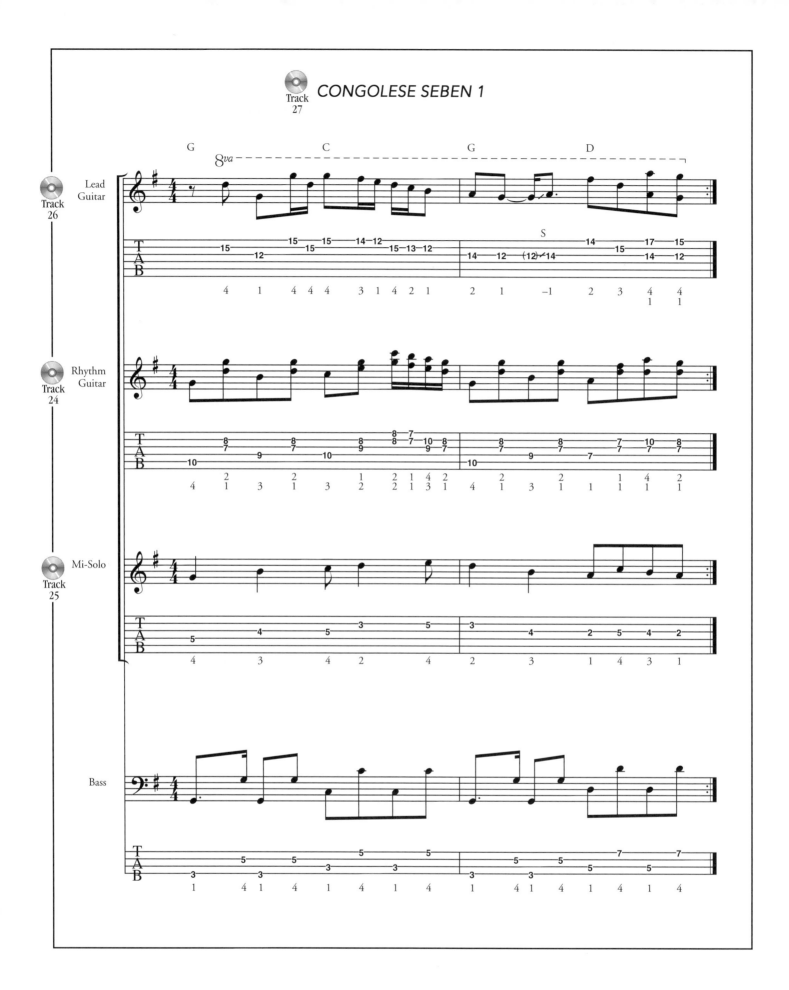

CONGOLESE SEBEN 2

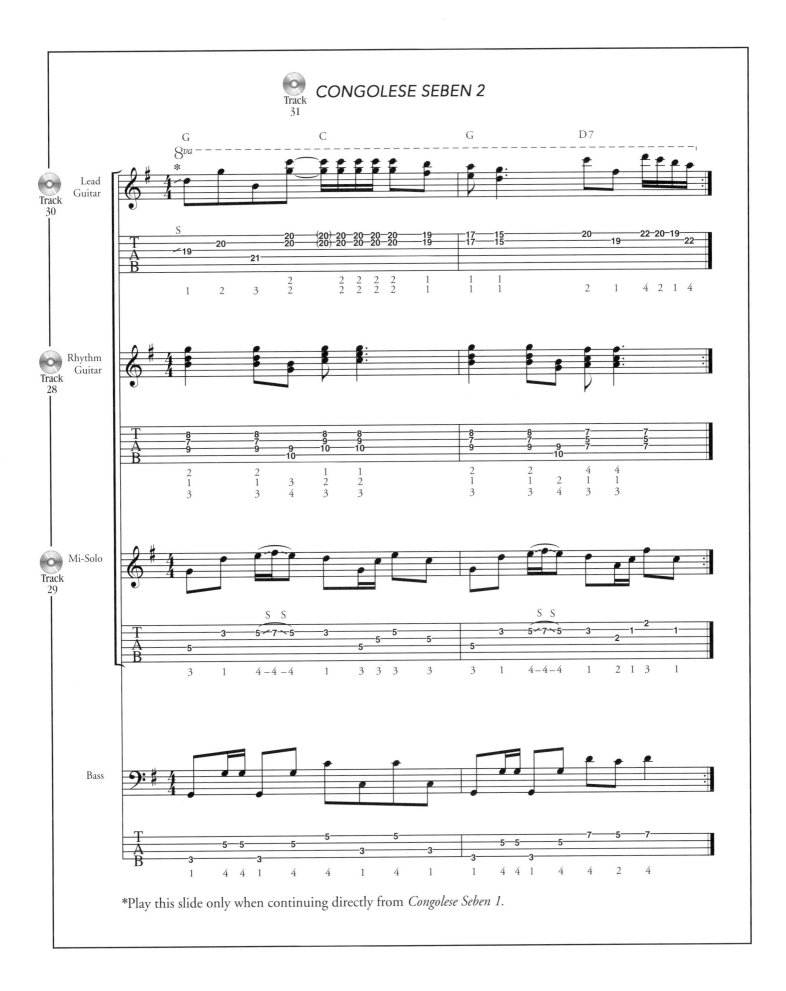

*Play this slide only when continuing directly from *Congolese Seben 1*.

Chapter 4 — MUSIC OF THE MANDING GRIOTS

AFRICA

Chapters 4 and 5 deal with prominent guitar styles of Francophone (French-speaking) Africa, especially Mali and Guinea. We start with the music of *griots*, hereditary praise singers and musical entertainers whose art is particularly developed among the Manding people of Mali, Guinea, Gambia, Senegal, Guinea Bissau, Ivory Coast, and Burkina Faso. Griot music is most centrally concerned with singing, typically recounting family lineages and the great deeds of revered ancestors. A singing griot— often a woman—is a staple at social ceremonies such as weddings and baptisms. Instrumental prowess is also very strong among the griots. There are three principle melodic instruments among the Manding griots: the *kora* (21-string bridge harp), the *balafon* (a wooden xylophone), and the *ngoni* (a percussive spike-lute believed to be the ancestor of the American banjo).

*The **kora**. Toumani Diabaté (born 1965) is generally considered to be the greatest living player of the instrument.*

*The **ngoni**. Basekou Kouyaté (born 1969) is known for his exploration of the instrument's links to American blues and folk music.*

*The **balafon**. Keletigui Diabaté (born 1930), here shown with an example of the instrument, was the first lead guitarist in Mali's national orchestra.*

Djelimady Tounkara of Mali is one of the greatest practicioners of griot guitar. Tounkara plays lead electric guitar for the Super Rail Band, which was founded in 1970 with the goal of fusing griot music with modern Afro-Cuban and other dance-band music. He is also a master of translating traditional kora, ngoni, and balafon idioms into an acoustic fingerstyle guitar style.

To play in this style, you need to develop some unusual techniques, so let's begin with a few exercises. First and foremost is the right-hand picking. As with rumba guitar, griot is a two-finger style, but now *i* has a more complex role. It functions essentially as a flatpick, picking strings in both directions. Some griot guitarists use a fingernail. Others pick with the calloused end of the finger, but this takes quite a bit of seasoning. Beginners are recommended to use just enough fingernail to get a clear sound.

Note Tounkara's right-hand finger position in the photograph to the right. The *i* finger is pointed back at the neck, almost parallel to the strings. It is held straight and moves only from the base of the finger.

*The great griot guitarist **Djelimady Tounkara** (born 1947), lead player of the Super Rail Band, won the BBC Radio World Music Award for Africa in 2001.*

Using the right-hand position shown in the photo at the bottom of page 18, practice plucking a single note up and down, beginning slowly and then increasing speed as much as you can. Concentrate on making the sound consistent. The listener should not be able to distinguish *upstrokes* (strokes toward the ceiling, marked ∨) from *downstrokes* (strokes toward the floor, marked ⊓). This takes practice!

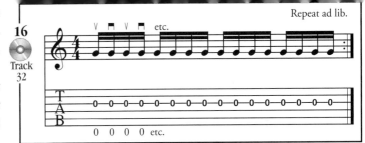

Example 17 is a C Major scale. Practice picking it with just *i*, using upstrokes and downstrokes as indicated.

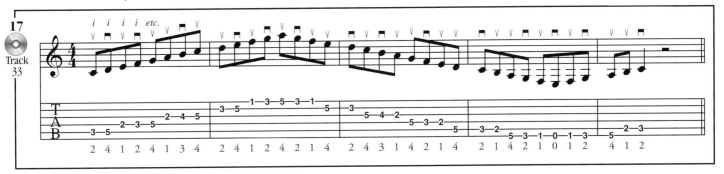

Example 18 is aimed at strengthening the downstroke played with the back of *i*. This is all played on the 1st string, and each downstroke is followed by a pull-off. As before, start slowly and work up speed.

P = Pull-off

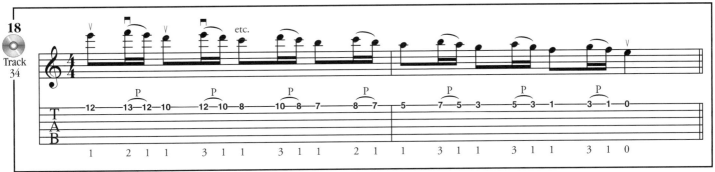

Both pull-offs and hammer-ons are crucial to the ornamented melodies in griot guitar music. Manding melodies often move downwards in groups of three notes. Example 19 covers all the strings from high to low in open position. Three-note groupings are used throughout, but the techniques used to play each grouping differ. In addition to pull-offs and hammer-ons, you'll use *dragged upstrokes,* in which *i* "drags" upwards across two adjacent strings. This exercise merits lots of time and concentration. The goal is to fine-tune your touch and timing to make all the groupings sound as similar as possible, despite the use of different playing techniques.

H = Hammer-on

KORA STYLE

The *kora*'s strings are organized in two facing planes, the notes of the scale alternating between the strings of each plane (left, right, left, right, etc.). Often, the player will play a note on one side, and then a note a half step higher on the other. The first note is immediately stopped, so that its role is more percussive than melodic, and the second note rings. Typically, the kora is tuned in F, so this technique often involves a stopped E and a ringing F, or a stopped A and a ringing B♭.

On the guitar, you can imitate this characteristic kora sound by fretting the lower note with the 4th finger and picking it with *p*. Immediately lift the fretting finger to stop the sound and, using *i*, pluck the higher note on the next highest string. The two sounds should be almost simultaneous. First practice this move in isolation, then add an open E, as in example 20b.

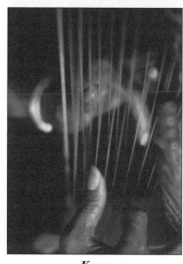

Kora

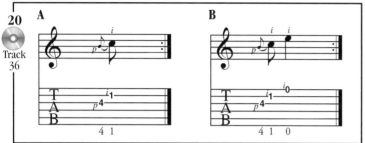

Here's the basic accompaniment part for the griot standard *Sunjata,* a song that tells the story of the founding king of the Manding Empire in the 13th century. Ringing and melodious in the kora style, this part is organized around two instances of the half-step technique described above.

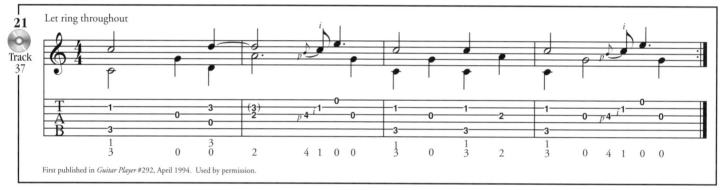

First published in *Guitar Player #292*, April 1994. Used by permission.

BALAFON STYLE

The *balafon* typically plays even, pulse-like parts that create a steady rhythmic bed for a piece. Though it can also solo dramatically with very fast, polyrhythmic riffs, its principal function is to create this even, rhythmic texture. Example 22 is a balafon part for *Sunjata* that consists entirely of pairs of repeated notes picked with *i* in a pattern of alternating upstrokes and downstrokes.

First published in *Guitar Player #292*, April 1994. Used by permission.

NGONI STYLE

The small *ngoni* lute often plays a fast counter-rhythm for the main part of a piece. When soloing, the ngoni can also add notes outside the key, something the fixed-pitch kora and balafon cannot do. Here are two parts for another traditional griot tune, *Keme Burema,* which celebrates a 19th-century African general who fought the French. The kora-style part (track 39) is fairly straightforward. The ngoni part (track 40) provides an accompaniment with a quick, contrasting rhythm.

KEME BUREMA

Track 41

Track 39 — Kora

Track 40 — Ngoni

Here's a version of the popular griot wedding standard *Diaoura*. It begins with a somewhat challenging ngoni-style introduction. Notice the chromatic notes (B♭ and E♭) in the triplet figures. These clearly show that ngoni is the model for this piece, since, in the key of C, neither the kora nor the balafon have these notes.

The intro is played twice. The first time through, take the *first ending* (marked by "1" plus a bracket) and go back to the repeat sign near the beginning; the second time through, skip the first ending and play the *second ending* (marked by "2" plus a bracket), which begins the main body of the song. Play the main body four times, then play the variation just once. *D.S. al Coda* tells you to go back to the sign (𝄋) and play from there. After playing the main body four more times, go directly to the coda, which is a slightly changed version of the intro. The intro is more difficult than the main body. If you have trouble, learn the main body first and take your time with the intro.

Example 23 can be used either as a variation on the main part of *Diaoura* or as an accompaniment that locks in rhythmically with the main body, as shown in example 24. This even, repetitive passage is more in the balafon style.

Griot Tuning

In standard tuning, most griot guitarists play either in C or, less commonly, in G, as well as in the respective relative minor keys (A Minor and E Minor). Though soloing can take the guitarist all over the neck, most accompaniments rely on C and G chord forms played in first position. That way, if the singer or another instrument requires a different key, the player can use a capo to change the pitch while keeping the same fingering.

Many griot guitarists use a tuning that raises low E (6th string) to F, and B (2nd string) to C. This effectively expands the guitar's range by placing a very low bass tonic at the bottom and moving melodic activity to the highest two strings. All of the traditional pieces played in standard tuning can also be played in griot tuning, with appropriate changes in fingering.

Example 25, a kora-style accompaniment for the song used to honor the original griot family, the Kouyatés, uses this tuning. Notice that it uses the same half-step kora technique found in the kora-style part for *Sunjata*, which you learned in example 21 (page 20).

23

Lydian Mode

Though the examples we've looked at in this chapter use the major scale, Manding music also uses some other kinds of scales. One is the *Lydian mode*, which has the sound of a major scale with a raised 4th degree (♯4). Here's a simple accompaniment to the song *Kaira*, just to give you a taste of the Lydian mode.

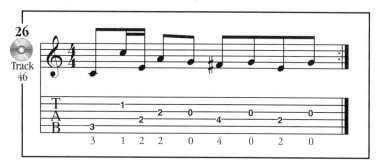

MANDING SWING

During the 1960s and 1970s, Afro-Cuban music fused with local traditions from all over west Africa, just as it earlier had with music of the Congo. From Senegal to Togo, great bands and singers emerged with African takes on salsa, in many cases giving birth to new musical genres. This happened in a big way in Mali and Guinea, where the new styles involved particularly innovative guitar playing.

When traditional griot was transformed into electric band music, Manding guitar came into its own. Djelimady Tounkara was part of a generation of electric guitarists who invented a distinctive style of griot dance rock. This style, sometimes called *Manding swing,* fused Manding griot melodies with the rhythms of Afro-Cuban dance music. Among the most famous of the electric guitarists was Sekou "Bembeya" Diabaté of the Guinea-based band Bembeya Jazz. Manding is just one example of the ethnic cultural traditions that Guinea shares with Mali, its northern neighbor.

Djelimady Tounkara playing with the Super Rail Band, which he joined in 1972.

Sekou "Bembeya" Diabaté was one of the original members of Guinea's legendary Bembeya Jazz, which he cofounded in 1961. "Diamond Fingers," as Diabaté was often called, is recognized as one of most important figures in the modernization of Manding griot music.

Manding Groove is written in the style of Mali's Super Rail Band, whose founding members include the guitarist Djelimady Tounkara. Play the parts with a flatpick. It may be hard at first to hear where the beat falls in the rhythm part, but it's very important to feel and play this correctly. As soon as you're comfortable with the pitches, practice this part with a metronome or drum machine to ensure rhythmic accuracy as you work up speed.

Coming in with the lead part can be tricky, so you might find the two-measure lead-in at the beginning helpful. The repeated quarter-note G will get you feeling the beat in the right place. Practice playing each part so that it locks in with the other; use the CD included with this book, or even better, have a friend play the other part. This will give you a real taste of Manding swing's unique rhythmic and melodic character.

Chapter 5 — MALIAN BLUES

The expression "Malian blues" has become a world music marketing cliché. Northern Malian guitar player Ali Farka Toure attracted international attention, in part because people around the world saw him as the John Lee Hooker of the desert. American bluesmen Ry Cooder and Taj Mahal have made forays into Malian music, most famously on Cooder's Grammy Award–winning collaboration with Toure, "Talking Timbuktu" (1994), and Taj Mahal's rich "Kulanjan" (1999), which featured an array of excellent Malian musicians. Given the obvious African roots of many American music styles, such projects make perfect sense and are important. But in terms of understanding Malian guitar styles, it's worthwhile to consider the music on its own terms.

*In 1999, **Kasse Mady**, **Taj Mahal**, **Ramata Diakité**, and **Basekou Kouyaté** joined forces for the first time to record "Kulanjan," a groundbreaking exploration of the connections between American and west African string music.*

"To me, blues is American music," says Lobi Traore of Mali, one of the bluesiest African guitarists around. "Nothing but American, not a music from here. We can play music that resembles it, but the blues is American. We should leave it that way." When Malian musicians categorize their music, they talk about Manding music—the sounds we looked at in Chapter 4—and *pentatonic* (five-note scale) music. Malian pentatonic music is a big category that includes the ethnic music of many distinct peoples: Bambara, Bobo, Fulani, Dogon, Songhai, Senufo, and Tuareg, to name a few. In guitar-mad Mali, each of these groups now has its own repertoire of guitar music.

Serious students of this music will want to delve into the cultures behind these sounds. For our purposes, though, we'll approach Malian pentatonic styles simply as music. The first thing to understand is that there are three main pentatonic scales: major pentatonic, minor pentatonic (very similar to the blues scale), and what some call *Dorian pentatonic*, which begins on the 2nd degree of a major pentatonic scale. (Compare Dorian pentatonic to the Dorian mode, which begins on the second degree of a major scale.) You can hear the distinctive characteristics of each scale by tuning your low E (6th string) up to a G and playing each of these examples against the defining drone of this low string.

 = Root

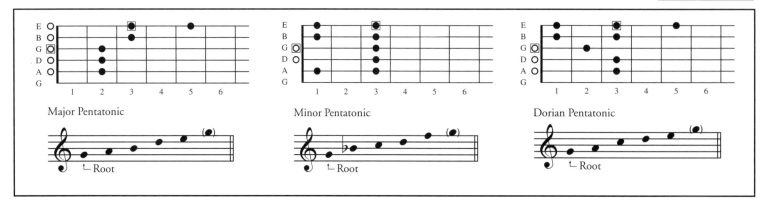

Major Pentatonic   Minor Pentatonic   Dorian Pentatonic

MAJOR PENTATONIC

Here's a fingerpicked major pentatonic piece in the style of a Songhai folk song from northern Mali. Ali Farka Toure plays a number of pieces in this style. Songhai guitarists favor the key of G and often tune the 6th string up to G, which you'll need to do for this piece. Play all the bass notes with *p*, and use *i* (all upstrokes) for the melody.

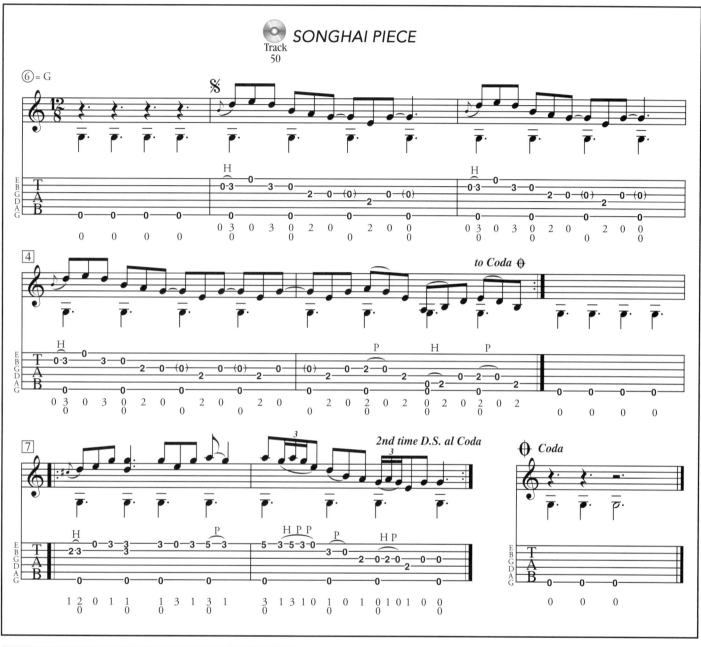

Ali Farka Toure, the Malian guitarist whose playing first caught the ears of American blues enthusiasts, recorded the Grammy Award–winning album "Talking Timbuktu" with Ry Cooder in 1994.

MINOR PENTATONIC

The minor pentatonic scale, which has a character similar to that of the blues scale, is found in much west African music. The tough, soulful character of minor pentatonic is unmistakable, whether it's used in Delta blues, rock and roll, or Bambara music from Mali. Bambara guitarist Lobi Traore grew up on rock as well as roots music, and he has made particularly effective fusions of Bambara and blues idioms.

Minor Pentatonic Duet has a west African, though not necessarily Bambara, sound. Play both parts with a flatpick. The accompaniment (track 51) begins with a four-measure introduction that uses an accented triple stop, a common feature in west African pop arrangements. When you play the lead line (track 52), make sure that it locks in with the rhythm of the accompaniment. In an actual performance of this piece (as is true of most pieces in this book), the players would cycle through the repeated part several times.

Lobi Traore *of Segu was dubbed the "Bambara Bluesman" when he began recording in the early 1990s.*

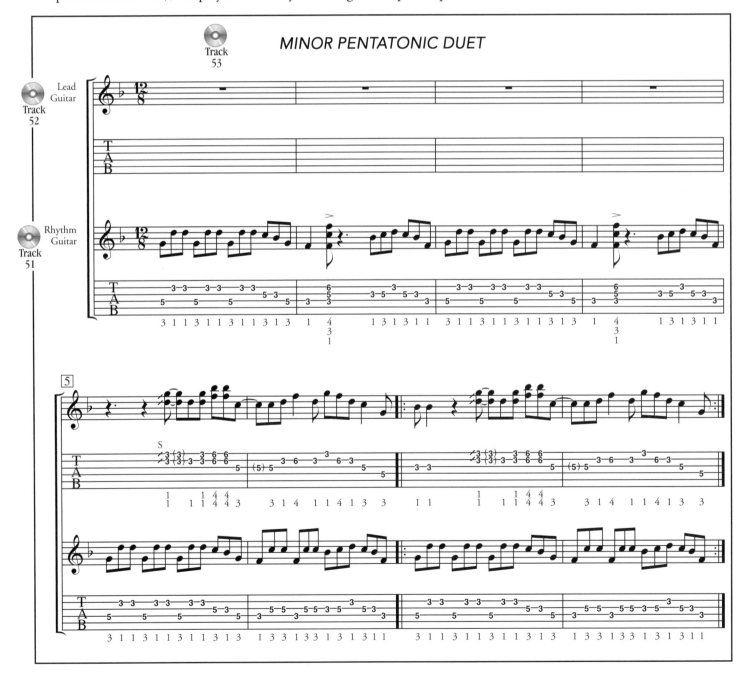

DORIAN PENTATONIC

The Dorian pentatonic scale has a particularly mysterious character. Since there's no 3rd degree, Dorian pentatonic doesn't have a clearly major or minor sound. Some of the most beautiful pieces by internationally famous Malian guitarists—notably Ali Farka Toure and Boubacar "Karkar" Traore—use this scale.

Here's a Dorian fingerpicking piece that approximates guitar music of northern Mali. The first section sounds against a repeating drone bass, picked with *p*; *i* does the rest, as in griot guitar music. Note the few places where you pick with the back of *i,* using a downstroke.

DORIAN DESERT BLUES

Before we leave the Dorian pentatonic scale, try this fairly typical fingerpicking pattern that's well worth mastering. Once again, the low E (6th string) is tuned up to G, and *p* plays a drone bass. The melody line, played with *i*, has a different rhythmic orientation, so be careful. Start by playing the bass notes, counting six beats for each one; notice that the pickup note of the melody comes in on the final beat of a measure. Once you can hear both parts together and make them flow, practice improvising within the scale. Try trading accompaniment and lead roles with another player. This is an open-ended example; improvisation, especially informed by recordings of Malian guitar music, is the name of the game!

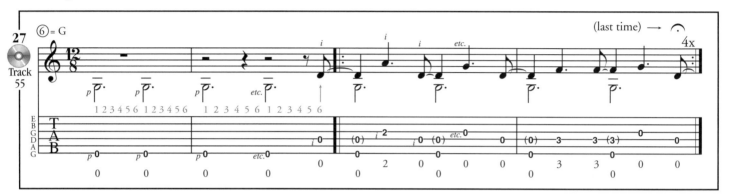

WASSOULOU MUSIC

Wassoulou music from southern Mali has funky rhythms and bluesy overtones that make it easily accessible to American ears. The wassoulou sound, popularized by singers like Oumou Sangaré, Sali Sidibé, Nahawa Doumbia and others, has found favor all over the world. There are many astounding wassoulou guitarists, though their names are not well known, even in Mali, where singers tend to get most of the credit. Many wassoulou songs are derived from the music of a six-string harp called the *kamelengoni*. A smaller, secular version of the *dosongoni,* a sacred hunter's harp, the kamelengoni is a relatively young instrument created in the 1960s. Today, the instrument is hugely popular, and its many innovative young players include Harouna Samaké, who has developed 8- and 12-string versions, and Benogo Diakité.

Example 28 is a kamelengoni-like accompaniment in the style of Bainy Koita, a session guitarist in Bamako, Mali, that you can play on guitar with a flatpick. Like much wassoulou music, this example uses the Dorian pentatonic scale.

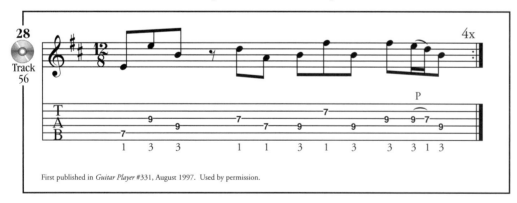

First published in *Guitar Player* #331, August 1997. Used by permission.

*The **kamelengoni**. Harouna Samaké, perhaps the most inventive and accomplished kamelengoni player alive, makes and plays 8- and 12-string versions of the originally 6-stringed instrument. He began his recording career with singer Sali Sidibé in 1993.*

Like most of west Africa's pentatonic pop music, wassoulou derives from traditional music, though it's now performed by electric and acoustic bands. Given the prevalence of kamelengoni, pentatonic balafon, and keyboards, most wassoulou groups use just bass and a single electric guitar. But wassoulou also works with two guitars, so try out *Two-Guitar Wassoulou Piece.* Start by playing the fairly typical accompaniment. Though chords are implied, this part doesn't lend itself to thinking in terms of chordal harmony. It's really a line, and no chords truly express its character.

Some wassoulou songs use $\frac{6}{8}$ and $\frac{12}{8}$ time signatures; the $\frac{4}{4}$ beat of *Two-Guitar Wassoulou Piece,* however, is more typical. The rhythm indicated in the percussion part is almost always used to accompany wassoulou. This rhythm is usually scraped out on a serrated metal instrument called a *karagnan.* If you don't have one handy, you can approximate the effect with a shaker or the hi-hat on a drum set.

Now add the lead guitar part. Use this notated version to start, and then try improvising over the accompaniment. Notice the way the melody begins on a beat different from that of the accompaniment. Once again, the rhythmic conversation between parts, a staple of African guitar music, makes all the difference—something to keep in mind as you improvise.

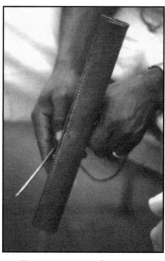

Karagnan and scraper

31

Chapter 6

SOUTH AFRICAN PICKERS AND STRUMMERS

AFRICA

South Africa has one of the most diversified music scenes of any country on the continent. It's home to a remarkable range of ethnic groups, each with its own musical traditions. South Africa also has distinctive urban music styles, ranging from the stomping township jive that emerged from places like Soweto, to the urbane, breezy jazz of Cape Town, to *kwaito,* the streetwise, hip-hop-tinged pop of today's urban youth. South Africa has long had powerful radio stations and an aggressive recording industry, so music gets around. The country also has a long history of paying close attention to cultural trends in the United States. While cities in central and west Africa went mad for Afro-Cuban sounds, South African urbanites were more impressed with swing jazz and country music, and later, soul, rock and roll, funk, and hip-hop.

In this chapter, we'll focus on just two aspects of South African guitar music: the Zulu fingerpicking style known as *ukapika,* and *mbaqanga,* the electric guitar pop style that influenced Paul Simon's album "Graceland."

ZULU FINGERSTYLE GUITAR

Zulu guitarists take inspiration from the drone-like mouth bow of their ancestors. The guitar provided Zulu musicians with the opportunity to add voices and to layer rhythms, and by the mid-20th century, the acoustic guitar had become their instrument of choice. Johnny Clegg, leader of the Zulu rock groups Juluka and Savuka, began immersing himself in Zulu culture at the age of 12 and never looked back. He explains that Zulu players tune the high E (1st string) down to a D and use it as a drone. Much of the action comes from *p,* which plays pulse-like, repeating melodies in the manner of the mouth bow.

Johnny Clegg (born 1953) founded the multi-racial crossover bands Juluka (1976) and Savuka (1987). He mastered Zulu language, singing, guitar playing, and dance, and became a sensation both in South Africa and around the world.

Look at the traditional *Walking Song* that begins at the bottom of this page. Start with the bass line, using only the thumb. Be sure to make it strong and driving. Then, try the variations that follow. Notice that each uses the same bass line, and that each melody is played with *i.* Work on the variations separately, then repeat and alternate among them in any order you like. The second and third variations, which include an accented double stop, will take some work to master. Those double stops should ring loudly, creating a strong counter-rhythm. Most Zulu guitarists have had to work with dead strings and beat-up acoustic guitars. They have to play hard to get a good sound, and this feature has become part of the style. If you play near the bridge, you'll come closer to the desired effect.

WALKING SONG
Track 60

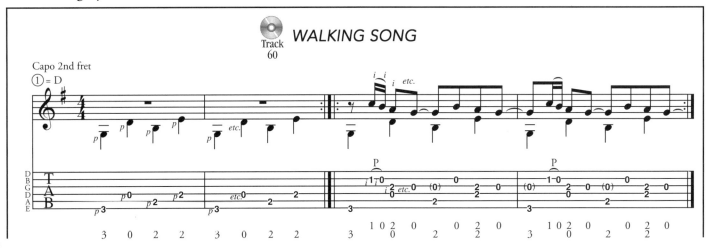

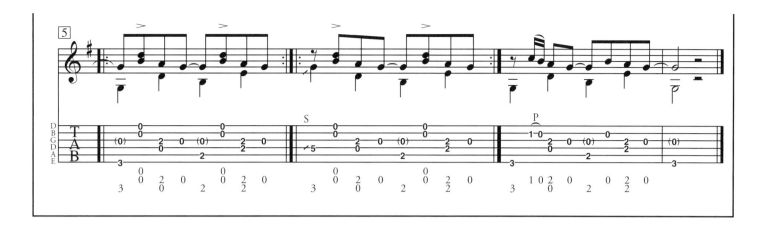

Here's another traditional Zulu song, one with a more lyrical quality. Once again, everything starts with the bass line (stems down), played with *p*. Begin by practicing this line by itself. Work it up to speed, then slow it down as you first add the melody—as Clegg describes it, "what the finger hears" over the bass line. When you get the two working together, gradually increase the speed.

First published in *Guitar Player* #226, October 1988. Used by permission.

MBAQANGA

Mbaqanga is the quintessential electric-guitar pop music of the South African townships. Developed during the early 1960s, it represents a fusion of the more jazz-oriented *marabi* sound of earlier decades and the new rock and roll and R&B that emanated from the United States. The mbaqanga sound came of age in the music of Mahlathini and the Mahotella Queens, backed by the Makgona Tsohle Band. Mahlathini, the great "groaner," sang low, growling leads over the Mahotella Queens' sunny, gospel-tinged vocal harmonies, while the band cranked out punchy grooves with squirrelly lead lines from the style's most innovative guitarist, the late Marks Mankwane.

Marks Mankwane, one of the most widely imitated guitarists in southern African music, was the lead guitarist for the Makhona Tsohle Band, which he cofounded in 1964. The band backed Mahlathini and the Mahotella Queens, the most successful mbaqanga act ever.

Some mbaqanga music is very fast, but *Mbaqanga Song* on page 34 uses one of the style's slower grooves. First, take a look at the bass and rhythm guitar parts, which set up the basic feel. Notice that the bass comes in halfway through the first full measure of the rhythm guitar part. Mbaqanga lead guitar is played in a flatpick style that uses lots of double stops. Mankwane and those who followed in his footsteps play cleanly articulated double-stop passages. Song intros often provide an opportunity for a guitarist to show off quick, sometimes complex riffs. In *Mbaqanga Song*, the lead guitar sits out for one bar, during which the bass enters. Two different lead lines, each of which can be repeated as many times as you like, are shown in the score.

Chapter 7 ZIMBABWE RUMBA

AFRICA

The rumba sound that emanated from the Congo beginning in the 1950s was hugely influential in east Africa. A variety of energetic rumba spinoffs developed in Tanzania, Uganda, and Kenya, where a style called *benga* emerged. Despite many local variations, one feature that remained constant was a greater equality of lead and rhythm guitar parts, resulting in rhythmic interplay that was often even more pronounced than that in music of the Congo.

By the time rumba trickled south to Zimbabwe, it had taken on the name *sungura* and inspired a string of top-selling, vocalist-led acts: John Chibadura, Leonard Dembo, System Masvida, and Alick Macheso. Zimbabwe rumba was also part of the mix for more eclectic Zimbabwe bands like the Four Brothers and the Bhundu Boys.

Take a look at *Sungura Stomp*. The clave rhythm that you learned about on page 13 is still implied, but now, the strong South African pop beat is more pronounced. Begin by learning the rhythm part, then move on to the lead. Notice that the introduction is played twice. As in Congo music, the drummer signals transitions back and forth between the A and B sections. As you listen and play, make sure that the rhythms of the parts lock in with one another.

Alick Macheso played bass in Khiama Boys, a very successful sungura band in Zimbabwe in the 1990s. Leading his own band, Orchestra Mberikwazvo, Macheso became the top-selling sungura artist in 2001.

SUNGURA STOMP
Track 67

Chapter 8   ZIMBABWE MBIRA

Probably the best-known guitar music from Zimbabwe is derived from the Shona people's *mbira*. This 22-pronged, handheld instrument is part of a family of African instruments often called *thumb pianos* or *hand pianos*. The most sophisticated of these is the Shona *mbira dza vadzimu*, literally "mbira of the ancestor spirits," because the instrument is used in religious spirit-possession ceremonies.

Mbira

*Mbira in resonating gourd, or **deze***

During the 1970s, pop groups began adapting mbira music to rock-band instrumentation, guitars taking the lead and accompaniment mbira parts, trap drums picking up the triplet rhythm traditionally played on gourd shakers called *hosho*. Singer and bandleader Thomas Mapfumo popularized the so-called *chimurenga* pop style, named after the guerillas fighting for Zimbabwean independence. In Mapfumo's band, the Blacks Unlimited, a series of guitarists have perfected the art of playing mbira rhythms and melodies on guitar. Two of the greatest innovators are Jonah Sithole and Joshua Dube.

***Jonah Sithole** (1952–1998), one of the key pioneers of the mbira guitar style, became lead guitarist for Thomas Mapfumo and the Blacks Unlimited in the late 1970s.*

***Joshua Dube** played lead guitar on Thomas Mapfumo's first mbira-related single in 1972 and continued to play with Mapfumo off and on over the years.*

Dube says that the key to understanding the complexities of mbira music is to identify the chord progression. Typically, this is a series of four one-measure phrases that repeat in sequence. Most mbira music is in $\frac{12}{8}$ time, so each phrase represents 12 beats. The progression in example 29 fits the song *Karigamombe*, the first tune most mbira players learn. As you strum this progression, which recurs often in mbira, notice that the rhythms in each measure fall into three groups of four eighth notes, giving the example a feeling that's closer to $\frac{3}{4}$ than to $\frac{12}{8}$.

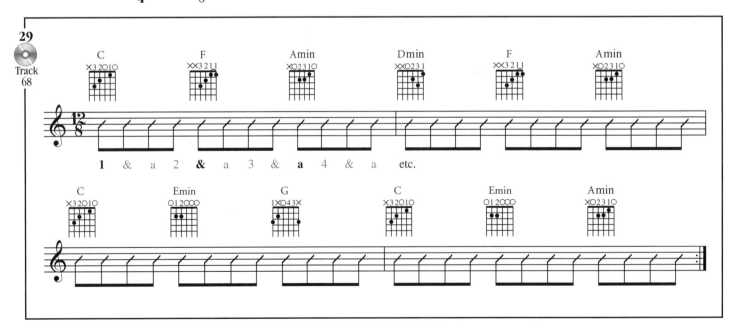

MBIRA FINGERSTYLE

Most modern mbira guitarists play electric guitar using a flatpick, but mbira guitar began with fingerstyle acoustic players. *Karigamombe Fingerstyle* presents the progression from example 29 (page 38) as a simple fingerpicking piece. Notice that the bass line, played with the thumb, breaks the 12 beats into three groups of four eighth notes. This progression appears in many Zimbabwean songs, though not always with this *harmonic rhythm* (rate of change from one chord to the next).

Note that if you emphasize the bass line, *Karigamombe Fingerstyle* will sound a bit like a waltz. When the drum part is added, however, the feeling changes. This drum part is a simplified version of the basic *hosho* pattern. Real hosho is ever so slightly more irregular, but this example does the trick. The 12 beats are divided into four groups of three, the closed hi-hat playing the second and third beats in each group.

As you play *Karigamombe Fingerstyle*, de-emphasizing the three-groups-of-four rhythm of the guitar and letting the four-groups-of-three drum rhythm determine the feel, you'll start to get the characteristic swing of mbira music. If you're playing it right, you'll get both a three *and* a four feel. In fact, mbira and mbira guitar parts get their characteristic sound by combining phrases in these two feels to create a complex, polyrhythmic texture that is quintessentially African.

FLATPICK MBIRA GUITAR

Below is an arrangement of the traditional song *Pidigori,* which uses the *Karigamombe* progression with a different harmonic rhythm. The first and second chords in each measure get three beats each, while the third chord gets six beats. The lead melody is taken directly from the mbira original.

The rhythm part, in the style of Joshua Dube, is more typical of an accompaniment in a band arrangement. As you play this part, you can slightly mute the strings with the side of your right hand pressing on the bridge. This is the way some guitarists approximate the timbre of the mbira.

Note that the picking pattern in both of these parts begins with an upstroke. This is often the case in mbira guitar lines. Since these lines start on weak beats, putting the downstroke on the strong beat helps you to get the feel. You may also note that Dube's accompaniment treats the harmonic rhythm a little differently. In many musical styles this would create a clash; here, there's no conflict. Though harmonic movement can be useful in understanding this music, it may unfold more freely in mbira than it does in other styles.

The bass line is in the style of the one used on Thomas Mapfumo's original 1980 recording of the song. The long pauses capture the character of mbira bass lines, which tend to follow rather than lead the melodies.

LEAD MBIRA GUITAR

Here's an extended lead guitar line that works with *Pidigori*. It begins with a figure used often in Zimbabwean guitar music: a descending line in alternation with a higher, unchanging note.

TAIREVA

As in west African griot music, traditional mbira songs are often rewritten as pop songs. Many pop songs use the *Karigamombe* progression, which you can think of much as you would the 12-bar blues—as much a form as a composition. *Taireva* is another traditional mbira song frequently adapted in contemporary compositions, as in the versions on this page and on page 43. Notice that both versions are built around G, though F♮ is included. You can think of *Taireva* as being in the *Mixolydian mode* (G–A–B–C–D–E–F–G), like much Western rock music.

The basic mbira melody works well both as a lead, as in *Taireva (Version 1)*, and as an accompaniment, as in *Taireva (Version 2)* on page 43. You may notice that the chord progression of the harmony part in *Taireva (Version 1)* is different than the *Karigamombe* progression. Mbira guitarists usually don't play chords, but all rules get broken. The lead line for *Taireva (Version 2)* is closer to the style of the late Jonah Sithole, a pioneer in the art of combining three- and four-beat rhythms in lyrical, flowing melodic lines. As you play the lead, let all the notes ring as long as possible. Note the F♯s in this part. You might expect them to clash with the F♯s in the mbira part, but, much as in blues music, they don't.

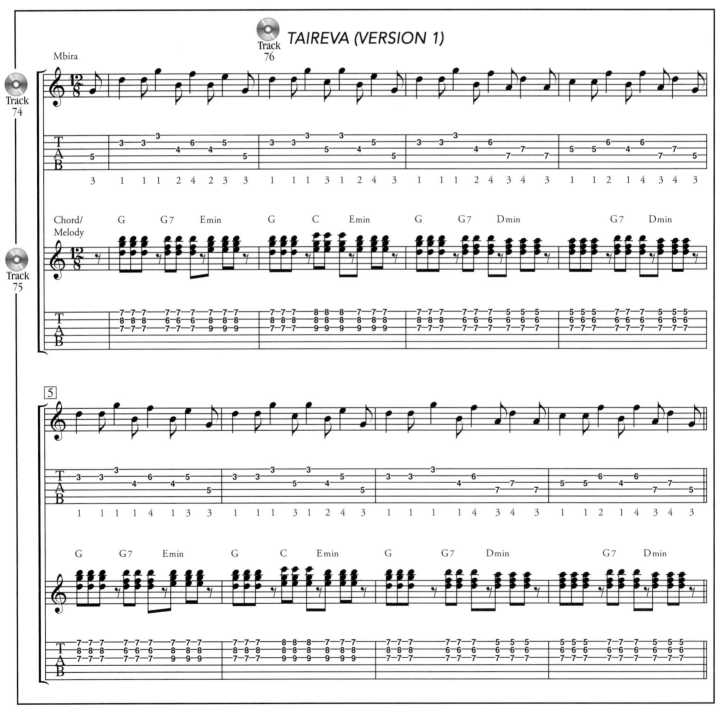

TAIREVA (VERSION 2)

Chapter 9   MIRACLES OF MADAGASCAR

AFRICA

The Indian Ocean island of Madagascar is home to many amazing guitar styles. In this chapter, we'll concentrate on some free-form fingerpicking music inspired by the island's unique array of traditional instruments. Among the most dazzling fingerpickers in Madagascar are D'Gary, Haja, and Johnny of the group Tarika Sammy. D'Gary uses more than 20 guitar tunings and a wide variety of personal techniques to capture the sounds of Malagasy instruments, especially the big box zither called *marovany*. Haja actually designed his own guitar, which he calls *guitare etouffée* (damped guitar). It has elastic bands he can roll over the base of the strings in order to damp the notes and make them more percussive.

Parallel 3rds are especially prominent in Malagasy guitar music. Instruments like the marovany and the *valiha*, a tubular harp, are strung a bit like the kora in Mali, with two planes of strings that let the player alternate hands—left, right, left, right—to play a scale. This arrangement of strings means that any two adjacent notes make a major or minor 3rd. Malagasy fingerpickers use *p* and *i*, as in many of the styles we've looked at, but they also use *m*, especially in combination with *p* in passages with parallel 3rds.

m = middle finger

*An array of traditional Malagasy instruments, including **marovany** (box zither), **valiha** (tube harp), and **kabosy** (traditional mandolin)*

*The **guitare etouffée** and its inventor, Haja (born 1965). Haja created a groundbreaking fusion of jazz and Malagasy roots music in the band Solomiral.*

Sammy's Vamp at the top of page 45 begins with an introductory flourish that leads into a simple two-chord vamp in the style of Sammy of Tarika Sammy. The vamp features a characteristic staggered Malagasy rhythm created by the sixteenth notes that fall on the second and fourth beats. The chord progression in the vamp is typical of Malagasy music. Notice that the vamp stays on F and G chords, though the example is in the key of C. This lack of resolution helps create a sense of restlessness and forward momentum.

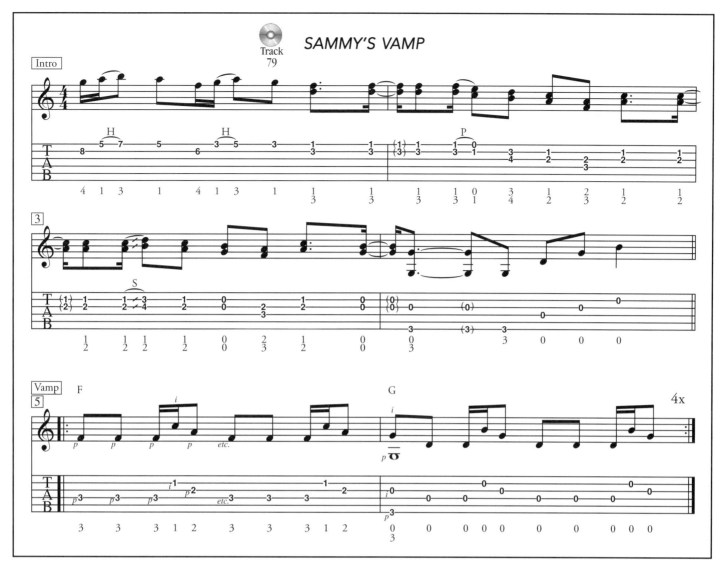

SAMMY'S VAMP

Track 79

Here's a variation on the vamp in *Sammy's Vamp* that works in a sliding 3rds lick. Pick the 3rds with *i* and *m*. When you get this under your fingers, try going back and forth between this part and the earlier vamp.

VARIATION ON SAMMY'S VAMP

Track 80

D'Gary (born 1961) emerged in the early 1990s as one of the most gifted and innovative guitarists in guitar-rich Madagascar. He evokes the character and spirit of Malagasy traditional music and instruments, but never imitates them.

Like a great deal of traditional and popular Malagasy music, *Malagasy Song* is in $\frac{12}{8}$. Fast triple rhythms are a staple in this music, but as you play *Malagasy Song,* notice the range of rhythmic possibilities that Malagasy instrumentalists explore within the confines of $\frac{12}{8}$. *Malagasy Song* also uses one of the most common open tunings on the island, in which E (6th string) is lowered to C and A (5th string) is lowered to G. This tuning increases the guitar's range, allowing it to more closely approximate a choral arrangement.

Additional Information

Listening is the best way to expand your understanding of African guitar styles. You are encouraged to visit **www.afropop.org** and check out the extensive discography listings and program streams available there. Meanwhile, here's a short list of readily available recordings that build on the material presented in this book.

Palm Wine
S. E. Rogie: *Dead Men Don't Smoke Marijuana* (Real World)

Highlife and Juju
I. K. Dairo & His Blue Spots: *Definitive Dairo* (Xenophile)
King Sunny Ade: *Odù* (Mesa)
King Sunny Ade: *Seven Degrees North* (Mesa)
Prince Osei Kofi and his African Heroes: *Sankofa* (Network)

Congo
Franco and TPOK Jazz: *The Rough Guide to Franco* (World Music Network)
Mose Fan Fan & Somo Somo: *Hello Hello* (Stern's Africa)
Papa Noel: *Bel Ami* (Stern's Africa)
Soukous Compilation: *Afrique en or*, Volumes 1–4 (Lusafrica/BMG)

Manding Griot
Bembeya Jazz: *Le dèfi & continuité* (Syllart/Melodie)
Compilation: *In Griot Time: String Music from Mali* (Stern's Africa)
Djelimady Tounkara: *Sigui* (Indigo/Label Bleu)
Djessou Mory Kanté: *Guitare sèche* (Popular African Music)
Mama Sissoko: *Soleil de minuit* (Tinder)
Super Rail Band: *Mansa* (Indigo/Label Bleu)

Malian Blues
Ali Farka Toure: *The Source* (World Circuit/Hannibal)
Boubacar Traoré: *Sa Golo* (Indigo/Label Bleu)
Habib Koite: *Musa Ko* (Contrejour/World Village)
Lobi Traoré: *Duga* (Cobalt)
Oumou Sangare: *Bi Furu* (World Circuit/Nonesuch)

South Africa
Johnny Clegg & Juluka: *A Johnny Clegg and Juluka Collection* (Putumayo)
Mahlathini & the Mahotella Queens: Any title you can find. All are good!
The Soul Brothers: *The Rough Guide to the Soul Brothers* (World Music Network)

Zimbabwe
Bhundu Boys: *The Shed Sessions* (Sadza/Stern's)
Compilation: Zimbabwe Frontline 3: *Roots Rock Guitar Party* (Earthworks/Stern's)
Thomas Mapfumo & Blacks Unlimited: *The Chimurenga Singles* (Shanachie)
Thomas Mapfumo & Blacks Unlimited: *Chimurenga Explosion* (Anonymous Web)

Madagascar
Compilation: *The Moon and the Banana Tree: New Guitar Music from Madagascar* (Shanachie)
D'Gary and Jihé: *Horombe* (Indigo/Label Bleu)
Jaojoby: *Aza Arianao* (Indigo/Label Bleu)

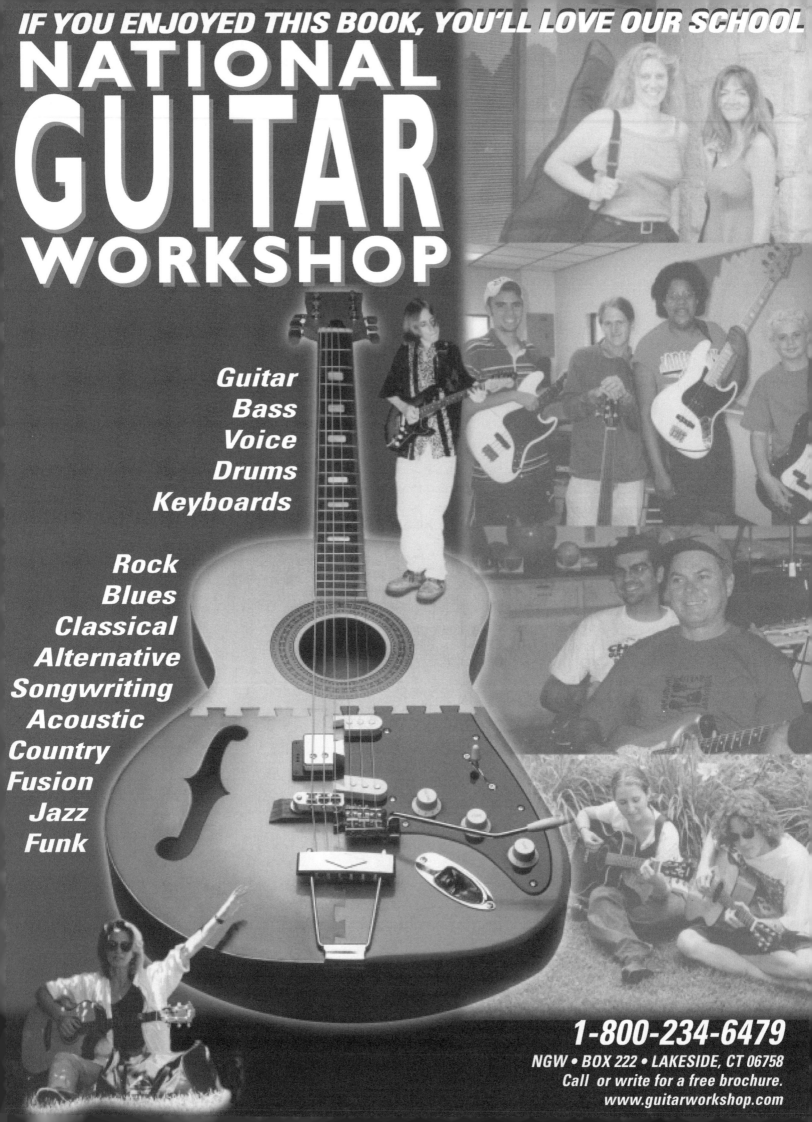